Joy to the World!

The Stories Behind Your Favorite Christmas Carols

KENNETH W. OSBECK

kregel
PUBLICATIONS

Grand Rapids, MI 49501

Joy to the World!
The Stories Behind Your Favorite Christmas Carols

© 1999 by Kenneth W. Osbeck

Published by Kregel Publications, a division of Kregel, Inc., P.O. Box 2607, Grand Rapids, MI 49501. Kregel Publications provides trusted, biblical publications for Christian growth and service. Your comments and suggestions are valued.

For more information about Kregel Publications, visit our web site: www.kregel.com

Cover and book design: Frank Gutbrod
Coverphoto: © by PhotoDisc, Inc.

Library of Congress Cataloging-in-Publication Data
Osbeck, Kenneth W.
    Joy to the world! the stories behind your favorite
Christmas carols / by Kenneth W. Osbeck.
        p.   cm.
    1. Christmas Prayer-books and devotions—English.
    2. Carols, English—History and criticism.   I. Title.
BV45.083   1999   242'.335—dc 21   99-16479
                                                                    CIP

ISBN 0-8254-3431-9

Printed in the United States of America

1 2 3 4 5 / 03 02 01 00 99

Contents

4   *Contents*

Introduction

What joy the glorious music of Christmas brings to our celebration of Christ's birth! No other season offers such an abundance of spiritual enrichment through song. Even though some of these musical expressions from around the world have been heard for centuries, they all fill us with awe and praise as we worship anew with the shepherds and angels of old.

These folk-song-like hymns confront us once again with the profound mystery of the incarnation: God became a humble Babe that we might live and reign with Him eternally. Who can fathom fully this amazing truth? Yet even amid all the glitter and commercialization that dominate our modern culture and tend to dull our spiritual senses, the singing of these simple songs has a way of recapturing our spirit's focus on Bethlehem's manger.

During each Christmas season in ancient England, it was customary in the various communities to prepare large sheets called "broadsides" for use in group singing. Perhaps this *Joy to the World!* collection can be your personal "broadside" this season as you gather with family and friends to share these treasured songs. You may also wish to organize caroling visits to residences of the elderly, hospitals, prisons, or homes of shut-ins—individuals who desperately need to hear once again the inspiring sounds of the Christmas message.

As you sing these timeless songs this season, perhaps you will wonder where and how the words and music began. What prompted the birth of such unusual expressions? Background material is given for each of the twenty-five favorites to enhance your festive joy, to aid you in "singing with the spirit and with understanding" (see 1 Cor. 14:15 KJV), and to remind you of the promise of God Almighty that "whoso offereth praise glorifieth me" (Ps. 50:23 KJV).

SO LET'S GO ON SINGING
*   these Christmas songs so sweet,*
Whose music cheers and strengthens,
*   and makes life more complete.*
In tune with all that's lovely—
*   God's angels list'ning near—*
In company with multitudes
*   who live in light more clear.*
Let's sing these songs so precious—
*   which Dad and Mother sang—*
With all the saints before them,
*   whose hearts with gladness rang.*
Yes, sing them soft and tender,
*   these songs God loves to own,*
Until we sing them grander still
*   with Christ, around "The Throne."*

—W. T. Keeler
Adapted by Kenneth W. Osbeck

1

Angels from the Realms of Glory

Come, let us bow down in worship,
let us kneel before the LORD our Maker.

—Psalm 95:6

Angels from the Realms of Glory

JAMES MONTGOMERY, 1771–1854

HENRY SMART, 1813–1879

"Regent Square"

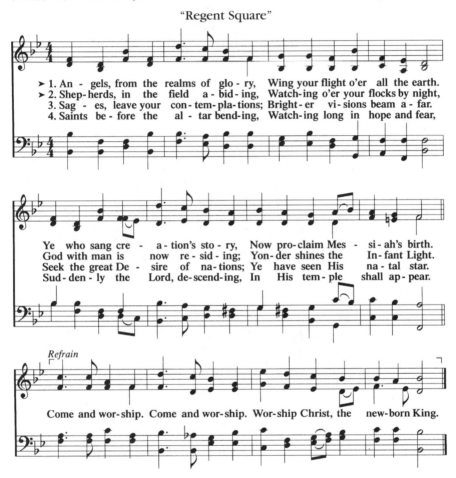

1. An - gels, from the realms of glo - ry, Wing your flight o'er all the earth.
2. Shep-herds, in the field a - bid - ing, Watch-ing o'er your flocks by night,
3. Sag - es, leave your con - tem-pla-tions; Bright - er vi - sions beam a - far.
4. Saints be - fore the al - tar bend-ing, Watch-ing long in hope and fear,

Ye who sang cre - a - tion's sto - ry, Now pro - claim Mes - si - ah's birth.
God with man is now re - sid - ing; Yon - der shines the In - fant Light.
Seek the great De - sire of na - tions; Ye have seen His na - tal star.
Sud - den - ly the Lord, de-scend-ing, In His tem - ple shall ap - pear.

Refrain

Come and wor-ship. Come and wor-ship. Wor-ship Christ, the new-born King.

*W*ith its vivid portrayal of various participants in the adoration of the Christ child, "Angels from the Realms of Glory" is considered by many students of hymnody to be our finest Christmas hymn of worship. In a unique way the text addresses first the angelic chorus heard at the dawn of creation (Job 38:7), then the shepherds in the second stanza, the wise men in the third, and, finally, all believers who faithfully await Christ's second coming to earth. The response of each group is the same—kneeling humbly in worship, which is the very essence of the entire Christmas story.

The author, James Montgomery, was known as a deeply devoted, noble person who made an important contribution to English hymnody through his approximately four hundred sacred texts. At the age of twenty-three he was appointed editor of the weekly *Sheffield Register* in London, maintaining this position for the next thirty-one years. Through this influential paper Montgomery championed many different causes, including the abolition of slavery. "Angels from the Realms of Glory" first appeared in Montgomery's newspaper on December 24, 1816. Later it was published in a hymnal titled *Montgomery's Original Hymns* and was known as "Good Tidings of Great Joy to All People."

An interesting stanza not found in most hymnals is this one addressing the Trinity:

> Lord of Heaven, we adore Thee,
> God the Father, God the Son;
> God the Spirit, one in glory,

One the same eternal throne.
Hallelujah! Hallelujah!
Lord of Heaven, Three in One.

The melody, known as "Regent Square," was composed by Henry Smart. Although largely self-taught, Smart was recognized as one of the finest organists and composers in the British Isles in his day. He was totally blind for the last fifteen years of his life, yet he continued to play and write some of his finest music. "Regent Square" was written during this period of blindness. The tune was dedicated to the Regent Square Presbyterian Church, known as the "Cathedral of Presbyterianism" in London.

————————————————

Just as the angels, shepherds, and wise men
all bowed their knees in the worship of Christ,
may we pause in our busy lives to do the same.
Worship Christ, "the new-born King,"
and the soon returning KING OF KINGS!

2

Angels We Have Heard on High

Glory to God in the highest, and on earth peace to men on whom his favor rests.

—Luke 2:14

Angels We Have Heard on High

French carol

French melody

1. An - gels we have heard on high, Sweet - ly sing - ing o'er the plains,
2. Shep-herds, why this ju - bi - lee? Why your joy - ous strains pro - long?
3. Come to Beth - le - hem and see Him whose birth the an - gels sing;
4. See Him in a man - ger laid— Je - sus, Lord of heav'n and earth;

And the moun-tains, in re - ply, Ech - o - ing their joy - ous strains.
What the glad - some ti - dings be Which in - spire your heav'n - ly song?
Come a - dore, on bend - ed knee, Christ the Lord, the new - born King.
Ma - ry, Jo - seph, lend your aid, With us sing our Sav - ior's birth.

CHORUS

Glo - - - - - - - - ri - a

in ex - cel - sis De - o! Glo - - - - - -

- - - - ri - a in ex - cel - sis De - o!

*A*s vast numbers of angels swiftly descended toward earth through the star-sprinkled sky, the leading angel halted them with a sign. They hovered with folded wings over a silent field near Bethlehem. "There they are," said the leading angel, "the humble shepherds who have been chosen by God to receive your message. It will be the most wonderful news that people have ever received. Are you ready with your great angelic chorus?"

The leading angel drifted slightly downward so that he could be seen by the shepherds below. They were terrified! They all covered their faces in the brilliance of the light but earnestly listened with awe as the vision before them began to speak in their own language:

"Do not be afraid. I bring you good news of great joy that will be for all the people. Today in the town of David a Savior has been born to you; He is Christ the Lord."

Instantly surrounding the angel was the brilliant heavenly host, and echoing through the sky and o'er the plains was the most beautiful singing that the shepherds had ever heard, exulting and praising God for the long-awaited gift of His Son. They made haste to see the Savior with their own eyes.

Although little is known of its origins, including the English translation, this inspiring eighteenth-century French carol has become a universal favorite. It was first published anonymously in 1855.

The Bible teaches that angels are the ministering servants of God and that they are continually being sent to help and protect us, the heirs of salvation. Two of their most important tasks were in the form of announcements: the creation of this world (Job 38:7) and the momentous occasion of Christ's earthly arrival.

---

*Join the angelic chorus by glorifying God in the highest
and by enjoying His promised peace as you sing
this joyous carol. Rejoice that God's angels
are concerned about you and are sent to protect
and care for you personally.*

*All my heart this night rejoices
As I hear, far and near,
Sweetest angel voices.
"Christ is born" their choirs are singing,
Till the air with joy is ringing.*

—Paul Gerhardt

3

Away in a Manger

And she gave birth to her firstborn, a son.
She wrapped him in cloths and placed him
in a manger, because there was no room
for them in the inn.

—Luke 2:7

Away in a Manger

1, 2 – Source unknown
3 – JOHN THOMAS McFARLAND, 1851–1913

JAMES R. MURRAY, 1841–1905

1. A - way in a man-ger, no crib for a bed, The lit - tle Lord
2. The cat - tle are low - ing, the Ba - by a - wakes, But lit - tle Lord
3. Be near me, Lord Je - sus! I ask Thee to stay Close by me for -

Je - sus laid down His sweet head; The stars in the sky looked
Je - sus, no cry - ing He makes; I love Thee, Lord Je - sus! look
ev - er, and love me, I pray; Bless all the dear chil - dren in

down where He lay, The lit - tle Lord Je - sus, a - sleep on the hay.
down from the sky, And stay by my cra - dle till morn-ing is nigh.
Thy ten - der care, And fit us for heav - en, to live with Thee there.

The shepherds had an angel
The wise men had a star
But what have I, a little child,
To guide me home from far,
Where glad stars sing together
Where singing angels are?

Christ watches me, His little lamb,
Cares for me day and night,
That I may be His own in heaven;
So angels clad in white
Shall sing their "Glory, glory,"
For my sake in the height.

— Christina Rossetti

*N*o Christmas song is more loved than this tender children's carol. With its simply worded expression of love for the Lord Jesus and trust in His faithful care, the hymn appeals to young and old alike. It is usually one of the first Christmas songs learned in early childhood. Almost without exception, every child responds to this text and music. Yet its pleasing melody and gentle message preserve it in our affections all through life.

For some time, "Away in a Manger" was titled "Luther's Cradle Hymn." It was thought to have been written by Martin Luther for his own children and then passed on by German mothers. Modern research discounts this claim, however. Stanzas one and two first appeared in the *Little Children's Book*, published in 1885, listing the author as "Anonymous." Two years later the carol appeared in a collection titled *Dainty Songs for Little Lads and Lasses* by James R. Murray, who apparently also composed the familiar tune. Murray was an American music teacher and music publisher. The precious prayer stanza— "Be near me, Lord Jesus"—was added several years later by a Methodist minister, Dr. John T. McFarland, for use at a children's Christmas program. Regardless of the uncertainty of much of its origin, this charming carol never fails to impress us with the true meaning of Bethlehem's humble manger.

How important it is that we take time to help our children see beyond the glitter and gifts of the Christmas season and to teach them the true meaning of Christ's birth. The most thrilling story ever known began in Bethlehem's manger some two thousand years ago.

———————————————

Use this season to enjoy times of family worship.
Include the reading of the Christmas story from Luke 2:1–20
(perhaps in different versions), share personal insights
from the story, dramatize the various events,
sing and play the carols (perhaps memorize key verses),
pray together, and discuss how the family
could share its joy with others.

4

Go, Tell It on the Mountain

You who bring good tidings to Zion, go up on
a high mountain. You who bring good tidings
to Jerusalem, lift up your voice with a shout, lift it up,
do not be afraid; say to the towns of Judah,
"HERE IS YOUR GOD!"

—Isaiah 40:9

Go, Tell It on the Mountain

Traditional

Traditional spiritual

Go tell it on the moun-tain, O-ver the hills and ev - 'ry-where—

Fine

Go tell it on the moun-tain That Je-sus Christ is born!

1. While shep-herds kept their watch-ing O'er si-lent flocks by night,
2. The shep-herds feared and trem-bled When lo! a-bove the earth
3. Down in a low-ly man-ger The hum-ble Christ was born,

D.C.

Be - hold, thru-out the heav-ens There shone a ho - ly light.
Rang out the an-gel cho-rus That hailed our Sav - ior's birth.
And God sent us sal - va-tion That bless - ed Christ-mas morn.

*F*or many people, another Christmas season is merely a rerun of the trivial and the sentimental. But for the devoted Christian, Christmas is much more than a once-a-year celebration. It is a fresh awareness that a Deliverer was sent from the ivory palaces of heaven to become personally involved in the redemption and affairs of the human race. The impact of this realization becomes a strong motivation to share the Good News with desperate people who need to know that there is an Immanuel available who can meet their every necessity. People everywhere must hear these glad tidings if they are to benefit from them. With absolute clarity they must hear the message, "Here is your God."

Spirituals had their roots in the late eighteenth- and early nineteenth-century camp meetings throughout the South, as well as in the active evangelical ministry carried on among African-American people during this time. However, few of these traditional songs were collected or published prior to about 1840.

Like most spirituals, the refrain for this one has no known author or composer. Spirituals simply evolved out of community life and worship. The stanzas for "Go, Tell It on the Mountain" were written by John W. Work Jr., a professor at Fisk University. He and his brother, Frederick J. Work, were early leaders in spreading and promoting the popularity of spirituals.

This song was first published in 1907 in *Folk Songs of the American Negro*. It is no doubt the best known of all Christmas spirituals. These traditional spirituals have become an important part of the American folk and sacred music heritage and are greatly appreciated and enjoyed by all of God's people.

Have I really celebrated the true meaning of Christmas
this year? How have I grown spiritually throughout
this Christmas season? What new insights have I gained
regarding this message? How can I share my faith
in the living Christ more effectively in the days ahead?
How will I proclaim unashamedly to a lost world,
"Here is your God!"

That your ways may be known on earth,
your salvation among all nations.

—*Psalm 67:2*

A story to tell, a song to be sung, a message to give,
a Savior to show—a gospel that must be proclaimed
as well as demonstrated.

5

Good Christian Men, Rejoice

Shout for joy, O heavens; rejoice, O earth;
burst into song, O mountains! For the LORD
comforts his people and will have compassion
on his afflicted ones.

—Isaiah 49:13

Good Christian Men, Rejoice

JOHN MASON NEALE, 1818–1866

Old German

1. Good Chris-tian men, re - joice With heart and soul and voice.
2. Good Chris-tian men, re - joice With heart and soul and voice.
3. Good Chris-tian men, re - joice With heart and soul and voice.

Give ye heed to what we say: News! News! Je - sus Christ is
Now ye hear of end - less bliss: Joy! Joy! Je - sus Christ was
Now ye need not fear the grave: Peace! Peace! Je - sus Christ was

born to-day! Ox and ass be - fore Him bow, And He is in the
born for this. He hath o - pened heav-en's door And man is blessed for -
born to save. Calls you one and calls you all To gain His ev - er -

man - ger now. Christ is born to - day! Christ is born to - day!
ev - er-more. Christ was born for this! Christ was born for this!
last - ing hall. Christ was born to save! Christ was born to save!

*A*s this sprightly carol reminds us, Christmas should be the most joyous season of the year for all true Christians. Our lives should be filled with gratitude to God for the immeasurable love shown to us in the gift of His Son. In fact, we should be abounding with joy—"heart and soul and voice"! This ancient hymn uses frequent repetition to impress upon us that the birth of Christ won for us an "endless bliss" by opening the way to heaven and conquering our fear of death through His assurance of eternal life.

The festive spirit of Christmas, however, should not fade away as the holiday season passes. The joy and peace that Christ brings to our lives should enable us to be continually rejoicing Christians, regardless of the circumstances. The blessings that came to us on Christmas morn have illuminated our lives forever!

"Good Christian Men, Rejoice" is an unusual combination of fourteenth-century Latin phrases and vernacular German expressions. The original Latin text was titled "In Dulci Jubilo," meaning "in sweet shouting." This is now the tune name. Over the years German people added their own wording, making this a "macaronic carol"—one that combines two or more languages—and they used one of their fourteenth-century tunes.

"Good Christian Men, Rejoice" was later given a free-rendered English translation by John M. Neale, the noted nineteenth-century Anglican clergyman and scholar. Neale left a great legacy to the Christian church with his many translations, especially those of the ancient Greek and Latin hymns of the Eastern church. This carol first appeared in Neale's

Carols for Christmastide in 1853. In the introduction for this collection he wrote, "Carols are the gradual accumulation of centuries—the offerings of different epochs, of different countries, of different minds to the same treasury of the church. New carols must always stand the test of time and prove worthy of use."

———————————————

Determine by God's help to maintain the joy of Christmas in your life ("The joy of the LORD is your strength" [Neh. 8:10]). Begin by giving an encouraging word to some lonely person.

Joy is the flag which is flown from the castle of the heart when the King is in residence there.

—Unknown

6

Hark! the Herald Angels Sing

God was reconciling the world to himself in Christ,
not counting men's sins against them.
And he has committed to us the message
of reconciliation.

—2 Corinthians 5:19

Hark! the Herald Angels Sing

CHARLES WESLEY, 1707–1788

FELIX MENDELSSOHN, 1809–1849

"Mendelssohn"

1. Hark! the her-ald an-gels sing, "Glo-ry to the new-born King; Peace on earth, and mer-cy mild, God and sin-ners rec-on-ciled!" Joy-ful, all ye na-tions, rise,— Join the tri-umph of the skies, With an-gel-ic hosts pro-claim, "Christ is born in Beth-le-hem."

2. Christ, by high-est heav'n a-dored, Christ, the ev-er-last-ing Lord: Come, de-sire of na-tions, come, Fix in us Thy hum-ble home. Veil'd in flesh the God-head see,— Hail th'in-car-nate De-i-ty!— Pleas'd as man with men to ap-pear, Je-sus our Im-man-uel here.

3. Hail the heav'n born Prince of Peace! Hail the Sun of right-eous-ness! Light and life to all He brings, Ris'n with heal-ing in His wings: Mild He lays His glo-ry by,— Born that man no more may die;— Born to raise the sons of earth; Born to give them sec-ond birth.

Hark! the her-ald an-gels sing, "Glo-ry to the new-born King."

The word *carol* is derived from the word "carola," which means a ring dance. Carols, then, have long been thought of as an early form of sacred folk music, dating from the early Middle Ages. During this period they seem to have been an integral part of the early mystery and miracle plays, which were widely used by the medieval church for teaching its religious dogmas. The carols were sung as an intermezzo between the various scenes of the plays, just as a modern-day orchestra performs between the scenes of a drama production. Then in 1627 the English Puritan parliament abolished the celebration of Christmas and all other "worldly festivals." During the remainder of the seventeenth century and well into the eighteenth century, there was a scarcity of these carol hymns in England. Charles Wesley's "Hark! the Herald Angels Sing" represents one of the relatively few important carols written during this time.

Like many of Charles Wesley's more than sixty-five hundred hymns, this text clearly presents biblical doctrine in poetic language. The first stanza describes the song of the angels outside Bethlehem and invites us to join them in praise of Christ. The following verses present the truths of the virgin birth, Christ's deity, the immortality of the soul, the new birth, and a prayer for the transforming power of Christ in our lives. As one writer has observed about the Wesleyan hymns, "These hymns were composed in order that men and women might sing their way, not only into experience, but also into knowledge; that the cultured might have their culture baptized and the ignorant might be led into truth by the gentle hand of melody and rhyme."

The tune, "Mendelssohn," was contributed by one of the early nineteenth-century master composers, Felix Mendelssohn. The hymn tune was adapted from one of Mendelssohn's earlier works, which he wrote to commemorate the four hundredth anniversary of the invention of printing. Although other tunes have been tried with Wesley's text, the "Mendelssohn" has become the recognized music for this carol hymn.

For more than two hundred years, believers around the world have been enlightened and blessed by singing this classic carol hymn. It certainly has become one of the most popular in the English language.

Be so in tune with the exultant song of the angels
during this Christmas season that when others see
and hear that Christ dwells within you,
they will be attracted to Him.

"God and sinners reconciled"—the real meaning of Christmas.

7

I Heard the Bells on Christmas Day

And he will be their peace.

—Micah 5:5

I Heard the Bells on Christmas Day

HENRY W. LONGFELLOW, 1807–1882   J. BAPTISTE CALKIN, 1827–1905

1. I heard the bells on Christ - mas day Their old
2. I thought how, as the day had come, The bel -
3. And in de - spair I bowed my head: "There is
4. Yet pealed the bells more loud and deep: "God is
5. Then ring - ing, sing - ing on its way, The world

fa - mil - iar car - ols play, And wild and sweet the
fries of all Chris - ten - dom Had rolled a - long th'un -
no peace on earth," I said, "For hate is strong, and
not dead, nor doth He sleep; The wrong shall fail, the
re - volved from night to day— A voice, a chime, a

words re - peat Of peace on earth, good - will to men.
bro - ken song Of peace on earth, good - will to men.
mocks the song Of peace on earth, good - will to men."
right pre - vail, With peace on earth, good - will to men."
chant sub - lime Of peace on earth, good - will to men!

*H*enry Wadsworth Longfellow was one of the great American poets of the 1800s, the author of such classics as "Evangeline" and "Hiawatha." The cruel miseries of the Civil War greatly distressed the beloved poet. With heaviness of spirit he put his thoughts into words to create this fine carol, contrasting the feelings inherent in war to those traditionally associated with the Christmas message. Since he was the most influential American poet of his day, Longfellow brought fresh courage and renewed faith to many of his countrymen who read this poem. As a member of the Unitarian Church, Longfellow did not accept the basic tenets of historic, orthodox Christianity; he did hold, however, a strong belief in God's goodness and personal concern for His people.

"I Heard the Bells on Christmas Day" was written in 1864 for the Sunday school of the Unitarian Church of the Disciples in Boston, Massachusetts. It originally had seven stanzas and was titled "Christmas Bells." References to the Civil War are prevalent in the omitted verses. The plain, direct wording of the present five stanzas gives this clear message: God is still in command and in His own time will cause the right to triumph and will bring peace and goodwill once more. The beautiful chiming bells of Christmas reassure us of this important truth.

The personal peace of Longfellow's life was shaken again eighteen years after he wrote this poem. His second wife, to whom he was deeply devoted, died tragically in a fire. Her death devastated him. In his remaining years he continued to write, however, and some of his greatest works came during this period of his life. After his death, his bust was placed in the Poets' Corner of London's Westminster Abbey as one of the immortal American writers.

John Baptiste Calkin, the composer of this music, was a prolific American composer of church music and hymns. His many works achieved considerable popularity during his lifetime.

The lesson of Christmas is that the only true peace that can come to our lives externally is that born of God's goodwill internally. "For he himself is our peace" (Eph. 2:14).

"Peace on earth, goodwill to men!" This is the blessed
promise of Christmas. It is the antidote for any fear
or hysteria that may enter our lives. Let the glorious sounds
of Christmas remind you of this great truth.

O thou joyful, O thou wonderful peace
revealing Christmastide!
Darkness disappearing, God's own light now nearing,
peace and joy with all reside.
—Anonymous

8

It Came upon the Midnight Clear

For to us a child is born, to us a son is given,
and the government will be on his shoulders.
And he will be called Wonderful Counselor,
Mighty God, Everlasting Father, Prince of Peace.

—Isaiah 9:6

It Came upon the Midnight Clear

EDMUND H. SEARS, 1810–1876   RICHARD S. WILLIS, 1819–1900

"Carol"

1. It came up - on — the mid - night clear, That glo - rious song — of old, — From
2. Still thro' the clo - ven skies they come, With peace - ful wings un - furl'd; — And
3. For lo! the days are has - t'ning on, By proph - et bards fore - told, — When

an - gels bend - ing near the earth, To touch their harps of gold: — "Peace
still their heav'n - ly mu - sic floats O'er all the wea - ry world: A -
with the ev - er - cir - cling years Comes round the age — of gold, — When

on the earth, good - will to men From heav'n's all gra - cious King," — The
bove its sad — and low - ly plains They bend — on hov - 'ring wing, — And
peace shall o - ver all the earth Its an - cient splen - dors fling, — And

world in sol - emn still - ness lay To hear the an - gels sing. —
ev - er o'er — its Ba - bel sounds The bless - ed an - gels sing. —
the whole world send back the song Which now the an - gels sing. —

*N*o Christmas season would be complete without the singing of this beloved carol hymn. Since the text was first published in 1849, scarcely a hymnal has been printed in which it is not included. It was one of the first carol hymns ever written by an American writer. The carol is really a commentary on the blessedness of responding to the angels' message of peace and goodwill.

The peace of Christmas, proclaimed by the heavenly chorus, is one of God's greatest gifts to mankind. "God was reconciling the world to himself" (2 Cor. 5:19). This message of reconciliation involves us on three different levels: peace with God, peace with others, and peace within ourselves. It is this blessed concept that Edmund Sears wanted to emphasize in his unusual carol.

In the second stanza Sears stressed the social aspects of the angels' message—the hope of Christians spreading peace and goodwill to others who are burdened and painfully toiling. The hymn was written at a time preceding the Civil War when there was much tension over the question of slavery, the industrial revolution occurring in the north, and the frantic gold rush in California. The final verse looks forward optimistically to a time when all people will enjoy the peace of which the angels sang. Later, in the midst of the Civil War, Sears wrote in his diary, "Desperately, desperately does this great but war-ravaged nation need the healing power of the Prince of Peace."

After graduating from Harvard Divinity School, Edmund Sears spent most of his life in small pastorates in the eastern United States. Throughout his life he also wrote a number of publications that had a wide circulation. Though a Unitarian, Sears stated in one of his books shortly before his death, "I believe and preach the divinity of Christ."

The tune for this hymn, "Carol," was contributed by a rather well-known American musician of the nineteenth century, Richard Storrs Willis. Part of Willis's musical training included six years of study in Germany, where he became an intimate friend of Felix Mendelssohn, who was greatly interested in the young American's compositions. "Carol" has proven to be a worthy melodic vehicle for Edmund Sears's text as generations around the world continue to sing and enjoy this carol each Christmas season.

———————

*Just as the angelic announcement of peace was given
at a time of much turmoil during the heavy rule
of the Roman Empire, so today God's message of peace
comes despite life's stormy circumstances.
Allow the angels' song to restore your confidence in God's
sovereign leadership in this troubled world.*

9

Joy to the World!

Shout for joy to the LORD, all the earth,
burst into jubilant song with music.

—Psalm 98:4

Joy to the World!

ISAAC WATTS, 1674–1748

GEORGE F. HANDEL, 1685–1759
Arr. LOWELL MASON

"Antioch"

1. Joy to the world! the Lord is come; Let earth re-
2. Joy to the world! the Savior reigns; Let men their
3. No more let sin and sorrow grow, Nor thorns in-
4. He rules the world with truth and grace, And makes the

ceive her King. Let ev-'ry heart prepare Him room,
songs employ, While fields and floods, rocks, hills and plains
fest the ground. He comes to make His blessings flow
nations prove The glories of His righteousness,

And heav'n and nature sing, And heav'n and nature
Re-peat the sounding joy, Re-peat the sounding
Far as the curse is found, Far as the curse is
And wonders of His love, And wonders of His

(1) And heav'n and nature sing,

(1) And heav'n and nature sing, And

sing, And heav'n, and heav'n and nature sing.
joy, Re-peat, re-peat the sounding joy.
found, Far as, far as the curse is found.
love, And wonders, and wonders of His love.

heav'n and nature sing,

As one of the most jubilant of all Christmas hymns, this carol omits the usual references to shepherds, angelic choruses, and wise men. It emphasizes instead the reverent but ecstatic joy that Christ's birth brought mankind. For centuries hearts had yearned for God to reveal Himself personally. At last it happened as "the Word was made flesh and dwelt among us" (John 1:14 KJV). The entire Christmas season should be filled with solemn joy as we contemplate anew God's great gift, the provision whereby sinful man might be restored to live eternally.

This carol is another of Watts's hymns from his well-known hymnal of 1719, *Psalms of David Imitated in the Language of the New Testament*. In writing this collection it was Isaac Watts's intent to give the Psalms a New Testament meaning and style. "Joy to the World!" is a paraphrase of these verses taken from the last half of Psalm 98 (KJV):

> Make a joyful noise unto the LORD, all the earth: make a loud noise, and rejoice, and sing praise. . . . Let the floods clap their hands: let the hills be joyful together before the LORD; for he cometh to judge the earth: with righteousness shall he judge the world, and the people with equity.

Psalm 98 is a Jewish song of rejoicing at the marvelous ways in which God has protected and restored His chosen people. The psalm anticipates the time when Jehovah will be the God of the whole earth and Israel's law will be accepted by all the nations. Watts, however, has given the psalm a fresh interpretation—a New Testament expression of praise for the salvation that began when God became incarnate as the Babe of Bethlehem and was destined to remove the curse of Adam's fall. Isaac Watts first titled his text "The Messiah's Coming and Kingdom."

Isaac Watts wrote more than six hundred psalms and hymns. As one writer has stated, "Simply, he is the best hymn writer that there has ever been." Watts has been called "the father of English hymnody."

The music for this beloved carol is thought to have been adapted by Lowell Mason, an American church musician and educator, probably from some of the phrases in the numbers "Comfort Ye" and "Lift up Your Heads" from G. F. Handel's oratorio, the *Messiah,* first performed in 1742. This adapted tune became known as the "Antioch" tune; it first appeared in Lowell Mason's *Modern Psalmist* in 1839.

Through the combined talents of an English literary genius of the eighteenth century, a German-born musical giant from the same period, and a nineteenth-century American choir director and educator, another great hymn was born that has since found a permanent place in the pages of church hymnals for use during every Christmas season.

What wondrous love is this that caused the Lord of bliss
to bear the dreadful curse for my soul. . . .
—American Folk Hymn

To him who loves us and has freed us from our sins
by his blood, and has made us to be a kingdom
and priests to serve his God and Father—to him be glory
and power for ever and ever! Amen.
Revelation 1:5–6

10

Lo! How a Rose E'er Blooming

But when the time had fully come, God sent
his Son, born of a woman, born under law . . .
that we might receive the full rights of sons.
—Galatians 4:4–5

Lo! How a Rose E'er Blooming

German carol
Trans. THEODORE BAKER, 1851–1934, stanzas 1, 2
Trans. HARRIET KRAUTH SPAETH, 1845–1925, stanza 3

Harmonized by
MICHAEL PRAETORIUS
1571–1621

1. Lo, how a Rose e'er bloom-ing From ten-der stem hath sprung!
2. I - sa - iah 'twas fore - told it, The Rose I have in mind;
3. This Flower, whose fra-grance ten - der With sweet-ness fills the air,

Of Jes-se's lin-eage com - ing As men of old have sung.
With Mar - y we be - hold it, The vir - gin moth - er kind.
Dis - pels with glo - rious splen-dor The dark-ness ev - ery - where.

It came, a Flow - er bright, A - mid the cold of
To show God's love a - right She bore to men a
True man, yet ver - y God, From sin and death He

win - ter, When half - gone was the night.
Sav - ior, When half - gone was the night.
saves us And light - ens ev - ery load.

$\mathcal{C}$hristmas is a time of miracles. The angelic chorus, lowly shepherds (the first recipients of the heavenly announcement), a humble manger as the birthplace of deity are all miraculous happenings. And the amazing wonder is that all of these events were foretold centuries before they occurred. From Genesis to Malachi, the Old Testament writers point to the coming of a Messiah, one who would reestablish a "son" relationship with the human race.

The prophet Isaiah is called the messianic prophet, he being the one who "saw Jesus' glory and spoke about him" (John 12:41). Seven centuries before our Lord's birth, Isaiah wrote of Christ's deity, His earthly ministry, His death, and His eternal reign. He described Christ's advent into the world: "A shoot [twig] will come up from the stump of Jesse [King David's father]; from his roots a Branch will bear fruit. The Spirit of the LORD will rest on him" (Isa. 11:1–2).

"Lo! How a Rose E'er Blooming" is based on these Old Testament prophecies concerning the "Rose of Sharon," an epithet for Christ (Song of Solomon 2:1). The German carol is thought to have come from the fifteenth century, when songs extolling the Virgin Mary *(Marienlieder)* were especially popular. (Note this reference in stanza two.) As Protestants began making more use of this song, the focus became more on Jesus than on Mary. As is true of most of our ancient carols and folk music, the authorship of this German text is unknown.

The music for this carol was harmonized by Michael Praetorius, a major German composer of the late Renaissance. Praetorius is recognized for his many sacred music works.

Theodore Baker, translator of the first two stanzas, was a German-born scholar who later became the literary editor for the G. Schirmer Company in New York from 1892–1926. Harriet Spaeth, translator of the third verse, was an active Lutheran musician in Baltimore, Maryland. She edited the *Lutheran Church Music Book* in 1872.

There is an interesting expression used in the first two stanzas: "When half-gone was the night." This no doubt refers to the long wait in human history for the "fullness of God's time" to happen. When it finally occurred, relatively few noticed. The third verse teaches a most important truth concerning our Savior's birth—Christ was "True man, yet very God."

For to us a child is born [true man], to us a son is given
[very God], and the government will be on his shoulders.
And he will be called Wonderful Counselor, Mighty God,
Everlasting Father, Prince of Peace.

—Isaiah 9.6

To the artist, Christ is the one altogether lovely.
To the builder, He is the sure foundation.
To the doctor, He is the great physician.
To the geologist, He is the Rock of Ages.
To the sinner, He is the Lamb of God
*   who cleanses and forgives sin.*
To the Christian, Jesus Christ is the Son
*   of the Living God, our great Savior.*

—Unknown

11

O Come, All Ye Faithful

When the angels had left them and gone
into heaven, the shepherds said to one another,
"Let's go to Bethlehem and see this thing that has
happened, which the Lord has told us about."
—Luke 2:15

O Come, All Ye Faithful

JOHN F. WADE, 1711–1786
CANTUS DIVERSI, 1751
Trans. FREDERICK OAKELEY, 1802–1880

"Adeste Fideles"

1. O come, all ye faith-ful, joy-ful and tri-um-phant. O come
2. Sing, choirs of an-gels; sing in ex-ul-ta-tion. O sing,
3. Yea, Lord, we greet Thee, born this hap-py morn-ing. O Je-

ye, O come ye to Beth-le-hem. Come and be-hold Him—
all ye bright hosts of heav'n a-bove. Glo-ry to God, all
sus, to Thee be all glo-ry giv'n: Word of the Fa-ther,

Refrain

born the King of an-gels! O come! O come, let us a-dore Him! O
glo-ry in the high-est! O come, let us a-dore Him! O
now in flesh ap-pear-ing!

come, let us a-dore Him! O come, let us a-dore Him— Christ, the Lord!

The songs of the Christmas season, songs about Christ's birth, represent some of the finest music ever written. For many of us, the Christmas season would be incomplete without hearing, at least once, the "Hallelujah Chorus" from Handel's *Messiah,* or perhaps a great classical work such as Bach's *Magnificat.* "O Come, All Ye Faithful" is also one of the universal Christmas favorites. It was first used by Catholic congregations before it was known to Protestants; yet today it is sung by nearly all church groups around the world, having been translated from its original Latin into more than one hundred other languages. The vivid imagery and flowing melody of this carol seem to have meaning and appeal for all ages in every culture.

The original Latin text consisted of four stanzas. The first verse calls us to visualize anew the infant Jesus in Bethlehem's stable. The second stanza is omitted in most hymnals, but it reminds us that the Christ child is very God Himself:

> God of God and Light of Light begotten,
> Lo, He abhors not the Virgin's womb;
> Very God, begotten, not created
> —O come, let us adore Him.

The next stanza pictures for us the exalted song of the angelic choir heard over Bethlehem's plains by the lowly shepherds. The final verse affords each of us the opportunity to offer our personal adoration to the One whom the apostle John describes in his gospel account as the Word

49

who was with the Father from the very beginning of time. Then each of these verses concludes with this invitation: "O come, let us adore Him, Christ, the Lord."

For many years this carol was known as an anonymous Latin hymn. Recent research, however, has revealed manuscripts that indicate it was written in 1744 by an English layman named John Wade and set to music by him in much the same style as used today. The hymn first appeared in his collection *Cantus Diversi,* published in England in 1751. About one hundred years later the carol was translated into its present English form by an Anglican minister, Frederick Oakeley, for use with his congregation. The tune name, "Adeste Fideles," is taken from the first words of the original Latin text; translated literally it means "be present or near, ye faithful."

———————————

Ask God to help you and your family make this Christmas season the most spiritual one you have experienced. Above all, worship Him—Christ, the Lord!

O Lord, grant that I may desire Thee, and desiring Thee, seek Thee, and seeking Thee, find Thee, and finding Thee, be satisfied with Thee forever.

—Augustine

12

O Come, Little Children

Let the little children come to me, and do not
hinder them, for the kingdom of heaven
belongs to such as these.
—Matthew 19:14

O Come, Little Children

CHRISTOPH VON SCHMIDT, 1768–1854   JOHANN P. A. SCHULZ, 1747–1800

1. O come lit - tle chil - dren, O come one and all. The cra - dle is here as in Beth - le - hem's stall. And see what the Fa - ther, from high Heav'n a - bove, Has sent us to - night as a proof of His love.

2. O see in the cra - dle this night in the stall, See here won-drous light that is daz - zling to all. In clean love - ly white lies the Heav - en - ly Child, Not e - ven the an - gels are more sweet and mild.

3. O there He lies, chil - dren, a - sleep in the hay, While Ma - ry and Jo - seph watch Him hap - pi - ly. The shep - herds are pray - ing be - fore His rude bed, Their sweet songs are sing - ing, by an - gels they're led.

*H*osts of singing angels and adoring shepherds hover about the crude cradle as Mary and Joseph gaze down at the peaceful baby Jesus. The hymn's simply worded description of the mystery of that holy night impresses even small children with the miracle of Christmas. We find no more tender expression of the awesome wonder of the nativity than in this lovely carol, written especially for children but enjoyed by all ages. The reminder in verse one that God's gift of the Christ child has given us a "proof of His love" should inspire a childlike response such as this from each of us:

> What can I give Him, poor as I am?
> If I were a shepherd, I would bring a lamb;
> If I were a wise man, I would do my part;
> Yet what can I give Him—
> GIVE MY HEART!
>
> —Christina Rossetti

It is so easy for us to lose the trusting simplicity of childhood. Yet we are reminded of the words of Jesus recorded in Matthew 18:3: "I tell you the truth, unless you change and become like little children, you will never enter the kingdom of heaven."

"O Come, Little Children" was written by Christoph von Schmidt, a German pastor and teacher who was known for his many fine books on religion and morals for children. The singable melody, with its appealing lilt, was composed by Johann P. A. Schulz. As a respected composer of operas and instrumental music, he served as director of music for Prince Henry of Prussia and also the king of Denmark. The hymn has always been a favorite of children in Germany, but it did not appear in English until 1946 in *Hymns for the Primary Workshop,* Westminster Press. The translator is unknown.

May the singing of this carol help us to celebrate Christmas with a childlike simplicity of worship that is pleasing to God.

We would see Jesus; lo! His star is shining
Above the stable while the angels sing;
There in a manger on the hay reclining;
Haste, let us lay our gifts before the King.
                                                    —J. Edgar Park

13

O Come,
O Come,
Emmanuel

All this took place to fulfill what the Lord had said
through the prophet: "The virgin will be with child
and will give birth to a son, and they will call him
Immanuel"—which means, "God with us."
—Matthew 1:22–23

O Come, O Come, Emmanuel

Trans. JOHN M. NEALE, 1818–1866

Latin hymn, c. 13th century

Unison

1. O come, O come, Em - man - u - el, And ran - som cap - tive
2. O come, Thou Rod of Jes - se, free Thine own from Sa - tan's
3. O come, Thou Day-spring, come and cheer Our spir - its by Thine
4. O come, Thou Key of Da - vid, come, And o - pen wide our
5. O come, De - sire of na - tions, bind All peo - ples in one

Is - ra - el, That mourns in lone - ly ex - ile here
tyr - an - ny; From depths of hell Thy peo - ple save
ad - vent here; And drive a - way the shades of night,
heav'n - ly home; Make safe the way that leads on high,
heart and mind; Bid en - vy, strife and quar - rels cease;

Un - til the Son of God ap - pear.
And give them vic - t'ry o'er the grave.
And pierce the clouds and bring us light! Re - joice! re - joice! Em-
And close the path to mis - er - y.
Fill all the world with heav - en's peace.

man - u - el Shall come to thee, O Is - ra - el! A - men.

The preparation for the celebration of our Lord's birth begins four Sundays before Christmas Day, a period known as the Advent season. The traditional church color for this season is purple, symbolic of the promised Messiah's royalty. Many churches, as well as Christian families, observe and prepare for Christ's birth by lighting a new candle on each of the four Sundays preceding Christmas Day.

The Advent season centers on the Old Testament prophecies concerning a coming Messiah-Deliverer. The Messiah's promised coming was foretold seven centuries before Christ's birth. At the time, the Jewish people were living in captivity in Babylon. For generations thereafter, faithful Israelites earnestly anticipated their Messiah with great longing and expectation, echoing the prayer that He would "ransom captive Israel." Perhaps the bleakest period in Israel's history was the time of the four hundred silent years between the close of the book of Malachi and the opening of the gospel of Matthew. The Jewish hope of a promised Messiah was all but lost in times of extreme cruelty and destruction dealt to the Jewish people by such enemies as the Egyptians, the Syrians, and the Romans. But finally the long-awaited heavenly announcement came: "Unto you is born this day in the city of David a Saviour, which is Christ the Lord" (Luke 2:11 KJV).

The tragedy of tragedies, however, is the biblical truth that the Messiah came to His own people to establish a spiritual kingdom of both redeemed Jews and Gentiles, but His own people rejected Him. The good news is that citizenship in God's kingdom became available to all who respond with personal faith to the redemptive work of His Son—our Messiah-Savior.

"O Come, O Come, Emmanuel" was originally used in the medieval church liturgy as a series of antiphons—short musical statements that were sung for the vesper services during the Advent season. Each of these antiphons greets the anticipated Messiah with one of the titles ascribed to Him throughout the Old Testament: Wisdom, Emmanuel, the Lord of Might, the Rod of Jesse, Day-Spring, and the Key of David.

The translation of this hymn from Latin to English did not occur until the nineteenth century. It was done by John Neale, a humble but brilliant Anglican pastor and scholar. The haunting modal melody for the verses is also of ancient origin. It is based on one of the earliest known forms of sacred music—the chant or plainsong.

Christ came not only to be our Emmanuel—
"God with us"—but even in a more personal way,
to be God in us. Celebrate these truths with your family
in a meaningful way throughout this Advent season.

God is FOR us—that is good.
God is WITH us—that is better.
God is IN us—that is best!

14

O Holy Night!

*So the holy one to be born will be called
the Son of God.*

—Luke 1:35

O Holy Night!

JOHN S. DWIGHT, 1813–1893

ADOLPHE ADAM, 1803–1856

1. O ho-ly night! the stars are bright-ly shin - ing, It is the
2. Led by the light of faith se - rene - ly beam - ing, With glow-ing
3. Tru - ly He taught us to love one an - oth - er; His law is

night of the dear Sav-ior's birth; Long lay the world in
hearts by His cra - dle we stand; So led by light of a
love and His gos - pel is peace; Chains shall He break, for the

sin and er - ror pin - ing, Till He ap - peared and the soul felt its worth.
star sweet - ly gleam-ing, Here came the wise men from O - ri - ent land.
slave is our broth - er, And in His name all op - pres - sion shall cease.

A thrill of hope the wea - ry world re - joic - es, For yon - der
The Kings of kings lay thus in low - ly man - ger, In all our
Sweet hymns of joy in grate-ful chor - us raise we, Let all with -

The night was calm and peaceful with only the flickering light of a campfire in the darkness of the field. Nearby reclined a group of shepherds watching the flock of sheep resting around them. The danger of wild animals attacking the lambs was always a concern. Suddenly a radiant light burst from the skies above them! A shining angel proclaimed the miraculous announcement of Christ's birth. Instantly a great host of angels appeared in the sky, praising God. It was indeed a "night divine"!

What did this holy night of Christ's birth mean to humanity? This inspiring song reminds us that it brought to a weary world a "thrill of hope" and freedom from all oppression. It meant that we would have a friend who "knows our need" and teaches us "to love one another." Truly we should bow in humble adoration and proclaim "His power and glory evermore."

The words to "O Holy Night!" were written by John Sullivan Dwight who was a native of Boston and a graduate of Harvard University. He wrote widely on musical subjects and for nearly thirty years was involved in the publication of the magazine *Journal of Music*.

"O Holy Night!" was performed for the first time in 1847 at the Christmas Eve Mass of the church of Roquemauve, France. Immediately it became popular and was translated into various languages. It met, however, with initial resistance from many conservative church musicians who thought its dramatic style inappropriate for use in church worship services. Yet today the song is found in most church hymnals. Its popularity continues to grow.

Adolphe Adam was the composer of this favorite song. He was a boy prodigy who studied at an early age at the Paris Conservatory. His French operas gave him considerable fame, but "O Holy Night!" is still his best-known remaining work.

Keep us, Lord, from losing the awe of that holy night
when Christ was born. May our carols of praise
never become tiresome and old. May the thrilling sounds
of Christmas ever remind us of how much we owe
to our heavenly Father for His great gift of love
on our behalf.

O God our loving Father, help us rightly to remember
the birth of Jesus . . . that we may share in the song of the angels,
the gladness of the shepherds, and the worship of the wise men.
Close the door of hate and open the door of love all over the world.
Deliver us from evil by the blessing that Christ brings, and teach us
to be merry with clear hearts. May Christmas morning make us
happy to be Thy children and Christmas evening bring us
to our beds with grateful thoughts, forgiving and forgiven,
for Jesus' sake. Amen.
—Robert Louis Stevenson

15

O Little Town
of Bethlehem

But you, Bethlehem Ephrathah,
though you are small among the clans of Judah,
out of you will come for me one
who will be ruler over Israel.

—Micah 5:2

O Little Town of Bethlehem

PHILLIPS BROOKS, 1835–1893   LEWIS H. REDNER, 1831–1908

*T*his beloved carol is from the pen of one of America's outstanding preachers of the past century, Phillips Brooks. In his day he was often referred to as the "Prince of the Pulpit." His forceful yet eloquent preaching did much to combat the Unitarian movement, rampant throughout New England during his time. Brooks's many published sermons have since become classics of American literature. He is said to have won the hearts of people with his preaching and writing as few clergymen have ever done.

"O Little Town of Bethlehem" was written in 1868, several years after Brooks had returned from a trip to the Holy Land. The experience of spending Christmas Eve in Bethlehem and worshiping in the Church of the Nativity, thought to be the place of Christ's birth, made an indelible impression upon the young minister. Three years later, while serving as pastor of the Holy Trinity Episcopal Church in Philadelphia, Pennsylvania, he was searching for a new carol for his children to sing in their annual Sunday school Christmas program. The still-vivid memory of his Holy Land visit inspired Brooks, and he completed the writing of the text in one evening.

Brooks gave a copy of the newly written carol to his organist and Sunday school superintendent, Lewis H. Redner, asking him to compose a simple melody that the children could sing easily. Redner struggled for a considerable time to contrive just the right tune for his pastor's text. On the evening before the program was to be given, he suddenly awakened from his sleep and quickly composed the present music. Lewis Redner always insisted that the tune was a gift from heaven. The carol was an immediate favorite with the church's children, as it has been with children and adults around the world to the present time. It was first published in 1874.

Though a bachelor, Phillips Brooks was especially fond of children. A familiar sight was this important man of the pulpit sitting on the floor of his study as he shared a time of fun with a group of youngsters. His sudden death at the age of fifty-eight was greatly mourned by everyone who knew him. The story is told of a five-year-old girl who was upset because she hadn't seen her preacher friend for several days. When her mother explained that Pastor Brooks had gone to heaven, the child exclaimed, "Oh, Mama, how happy the angels will be."

In the same way that God's "wondrous gift"
came to Bethlehem—silently—so Christ comes
into our lives today and casts out our sins and fears
if we sincerely invite Him to do so.

The hinge of history is on the door of a Bethlehem stable.
—Ralph W. Stockman

16

Once in Royal David's City

He will reign on David's throne
and over his kingdom.

—Isaiah 9:7

Once in Royal David's City

CECIL FRANCES ALEXANDER, 1818–1895   HENRY J. GAUNTLETT, 1805–1876

"Irby"

1. Once in roy - al Da - vid's cit - y Stood a low - ly
2. He came down to earth from heav - en Who is God and
3. Je - sus is our child - hood's pat - tern; Day by day like
4. And our eyes at last shall see Him Thro' His own re -

cat - tle shed, Where a moth - er laid her Ba - by In a
Lord of all, And His shel - ter was a sta - ble, And His
us He grew. He was lit - tle, weak, and help - less; Tears and
deem - ing love; For that Child so dear and gen - tle Is our

man - ger for His bed. Ma - ry was that moth - er
cra - dle was a stall. With the poor, and mean, and
smiles like us He knew. And He feel - eth for our
Lord in heav'n a - bove. And He leads His chil - dren

mild, Je - sus Christ, her lit - tle Child.
low - ly Lived on earth, our Sav - ior ho - ly.
sad - ness, And He shar - eth in our glad - ness.
on To the place where He is gone.

*C*hristian leaders have always realized that music is one of the most effective ways of impressing young people with spiritual truths. Such was the conviction of this lovely hymn's author, Mrs. Cecil Frances Alexander, generally recognized as one of the finest of all women hymn writers.

Mrs. Alexander was born in Tyrone, Ireland. Before her marriage in 1850 to Dr. William Alexander, a distinguished Anglican churchman who later became archbishop for all of Ireland, Frances was actively involved in the Sunday school movement that was just beginning to spread throughout Great Britain. Frances always had a love for children and a desire to teach them sound spiritual truths through her poems and hymns. Two years before her marriage, Frances published a volume of hymns titled *Hymns for Little Children,* which possibly has never been excelled by a similar collection. It covered a wide range of doctrinal themes such as baptism, the Apostles' Creed, the Ten Commandments, the Lord's Prayer, and other biblical topics. More than one hundred editions of this book were published.

"Once in Royal David's City" is from that children's hymnal. It was written to teach youngsters the meaning of the phrase from the Apostles' Creed: "Who was conceived by the Holy Ghost, born of the Virgin Mary." Like all of her more than four hundred hymns, most of which were intended for children, the text is direct, easily understood, and related to Christian living.

After her marriage at the age of thirty-two, Frances continued her writings and concerns for Christian ministries. She became keenly involved with her husband's parish duties, and her life was characterized with deeds of helpfulness and charity. Her husband once wrote this tribute: "From one poor home to another she went. Christ was ever with her, and all felt her Godly influence." Those who knew Mrs. Alexander intimately often claimed that her daily lifestyle was even more beautiful than her lovely hymns and poetry.

The music for this children's hymn was written by an English choir-master and organist, Henry J. Gauntlett, composer of several thousand hymn tunes. The tune name, "Irby," is the name of a village in Lincolnshire, England. "Once in Royal David's City" first appeared in published form in Gauntlett's collection, *Christmas Carols,* in 1849.

A mark of greatness is the ability to make profound
truths understandable even to a small child.
How thankful we should be that through the years
talented Christians like Mrs. Alexander have left us
with such a rich heritage of spiritual expressions
that are still beneficial and enjoyable today.

17

Ring the Bells

That your ways may be known on earth,
your salvation among all nations.
—Psalm 67:2

Ring the Bells

HARRY BOLLBACK, 1925–

HARRY BOLLBACK, 1925–

Ring the bells, ring the bells, Let the whole world know Christ was born in

Beth - le - hem Man-y years a - go: Born to die that man might live,

Came to earth new life to give, Born of Ma - ry, born so low,

Man-y years a - go. God the Fa - ther gave His Son, Gave His own be -

lov - ed One To this wick - ed, sin - ful earth, To bring man-kind His

love, new birth: Ring the bells, ring the bells, Let the whole world know

Christ the Sav - ior lives to - day As He did so long a - go!

The chiming of melodious bells at Christmastime is always a festive part of the season's celebration. But to Harry Bollback, author and composer of this hymn, bells also seemed to be ringing out a special message of Christ's birth as he heard their sounds one Christmas in São Paulo, Brazil. To their rhythmic and musical peeling, thoughtful, challenging words were quickly added to complete this inspiring carol. Mr. Bollback remembers the experience in this way:

> I was waiting in a long line at the bus station in São Paulo, waiting for a bus to take me to visit a fellow missionary, Paul Overholt. It was Christmas time. The city was beautifully decorated. It was about six o'clock and bells were ringing everywhere for "the hour of Mary." The people all seemed so excited. In this Catholic country, where Mary is so adored and worshipped, my thoughts turned to the birth of Christ. Like a dayspring, words and music began to pour into my mind. I quickly found a piece of paper and wrote the whole song down as it came to me—still standing in line.
>
> I could hardly wait to get to my friend's house, so I could hear how it would sound. Paul was a singer, working with Youth for Christ in that country, and I wanted to hear him sing it.

When I reached Paul's house, I sat down at the piano and played it. Paul was really excited about it and was the first person to sing it. I had nothing to do with the writing of it. The Lord just gave it.[1]

A talented musician at an early age, Harry Bollback had wanted to become a concert pianist. Soon after his conversion to Christ at a Christian camp at age sixteen, however, he decided to accept Jack Wyrtzen's offer to serve as pianist for the Word of Life organization. Although he continued his musical training at the Philadelphia School of the Bible, Harry was convinced that God was calling him as a missionary to Brazil. In 1950, he and his wife, Millie, left for South America. Their service continued for twenty years, at times in the jungles of the Amazon, before they returned with their family to accept once again an administrative position with the Word of Life Fellowship in New York.

"Ring the Bells," composed during Harry Bollback's time on the mission field, was published in 1958. It was immediately well received by the Christian public and has become a favorite Christmas hymn of countless people.

May we not become so concerned with this life
that we fail to hear and appreciate the melodies of heaven
all around us and to be challenged to share the story
of Christ's love with others.

---

1. From *Stories Behind Popular Songs and Hymns* by Lindsay Terry (Grand Rapids: Baker Book House, 1990).

18

Silent Night! Holy Night!

Today in the town of David a Savior has been born
to you; he is Christ the Lord.

—Luke 2:11

Silent Night! Holy Night!

JOSEPH MOHR, 1792–1848

FRANZ GRÜBER, 1787–1863

1. Si - lent night! ho - ly night! All is calm, all is bright
2. Si - lent night! ho - ly night! Shep-herds quake at the sight;
3. Si - lent night! ho - ly night! Won - drous star, lend thy light.
4. Si - lent night! ho - ly night! Son of God, love's pure light

Round yon vir - gin moth-er and Child. Ho - ly In-fant, so ten-der and mild,
Glo - ries stream from heav-en a - far. Heav'n-ly hosts sing, "Al - le - lu - ia!
With the an - gels let us sing Al - le - lu - ia to our King.
Ra - diant beams from Thy ho-ly face, With the dawn of re - deem - ing grace,

Sleep in heav - en - ly peace; Sleep in heav - en - ly peace.
Christ the Sav - ior is born! Christ the Sav - ior is born!"
Christ the Sav - ior is born; Christ the Sav - ior is born.
Je - sus, Lord, at Thy birth, Je - sus, Lord, at Thy birth.

$\mathcal{U}$ndoubtedly the favorite of all Christmas carols, "Silent Night! Holy Night!" is loved by both young and old for its serene and beautiful portrayal of the Savior's humble birth. Yet when Father Joseph Mohr and organist Franz Grüber, two young church leaders, wrote the hymn for their own village parishioners, little did they realize how universal its influence eventually would be. It was while serving as an assistant priest in 1818 at the newly erected Church of St. Nicholas in Oberndorf, in the region of Tyrol, Austria, high in the beautiful Alps, that Father Mohr wrote the text for this beloved carol. Father Mohr had often talked to Franz Grüber, the village schoolmaster and church organist, about the fact that the ideal Christmas hymn had never yet been written.

With this thought in mind, and after he had received the disheartening news that his church organ would not function, Father Mohr decided that he must write his own Christmas hymn in order to have music for the special Christmas Eve Mass and to avoid disappointing his faithful flock. The story is told that earlier that evening Mohr had visited the home of humble parishioners, a wood-cutter and his family, to welcome their new baby. On the way home the words for "Silent Night! Holy Night!" first came to him. Upon completing the text, Father Mohr took his words to Franz Grüber, who exclaimed when he saw them, "Friend Mohr, you have found it—the right song—God be praised!"

Soon Grüber completed his task of composing an appropriate melody for the new text. His simple but beautiful music blended perfectly with the spirit of Father Mohr's words. The carol was completed in time for the Christmas Eve Mass, and Father Mohr and Franz Grüber sang their new hymn to the accompaniment of Grüber's guitar. The carol made a deep impact upon the parishioners just as it has on succeeding generations. The passing of time seems only to add to its appeal.

A few days later, when the organ repairman came to the little village church, he was impressed by a copy of the carol and began to promote it all around the region of Tyrol. Before long, "Silent Night! Holy Night!" was sung throughout Austria and Germany and became known as a Tyrolean folk song.

The carol was first heard in the United States in 1839 when a family of Tyrolean singers, the Rainers, used the music during their concert tour. Soon it was translated into English, as well as all the major languages of the world, and it has become a universal favorite wherever songs of the Christmas message are enjoyed.

Allow the peaceful strains of this much-loved carol
to help you worship in awe with the shepherds,
and sing alleluia with the angels because
of God's "redeeming grace."

19

The First Noel

And there were shepherds living out in the fields
nearby, keeping watch over their flocks at night.
—Luke 2:8

The First Noel

Traditional English carol

W. Sandys's *Christmas Carols*, 1833
Arr. JOHN STAINER, 1871

*A*lthough no Christmas season would be complete without the melodious singing of this tuneful carol, very little is known about its origin. It is believed to have had its rise in France during the fifteenth century. *Noël* is a French word originating from Latin meaning "birthday," a joyous expression of greeting to celebrate the birth of the Christ child. The song is thought to have been brought across the channel to England by the wandering troubadours. Especially in the west of England, the carol, featuring the spelling "nowell," became a great favorite for Christmas Eve festivities. This was when the entire village gathered for singing and celebrating the bringing in of the Yule log. At that time carols such as this were still thought of as popular religious songs and were meant to be sung outside the church rather than within.

The carol first appeared in published form in William Sandys's *Christmas Carols Ancient and Modern* in 1833. The rather unusual tune is worthy of mention. With the exception of the initial measure of each phrase, the entire melody lies between the third of the scale and the upper octave. Some have suggested that this melodic line with its limited range could have been a descant for an earlier hymn. The harmonization of this tune was done by John Stainer (1840–1901), a noted English composer of sacred music. Stainer is best remembered today for his cantata *Crucifixion,* which contained the beloved anthem "God So Loved the World," published in 1887.

"The First Noel" portrays in vivid narrative style the story of Christ's birth, with all six verses needed to complete the entire event. The second stanza is often cited as being unscriptural since it is never stated in the biblical account that the shepherds saw the guiding star. The sixth stanza urges us to join together to sing praises to God for the marvels of His creation and for the salvation provided through Christ's shed blood. The repetition of the joyous "noel" in the refrain is equivalent to our singing "happy birthday" to someone.

It is interesting to observe that the "King of Israel" was first announced to "certain poor shepherds" only, but in the final stanza the phrases "let us all" and "mankind hath brought" remind us that Christ came to redeem the whole world.

Let's allow the joy of Christ's birth to be reflected
on our faces and heard in our glad "noëls" of praise
as we celebrate His birthday throughout
this Christmas season.

Fill me with gladness from above,
Hold me by strength divine;
Lord, let the glow of your great love
Through my whole being shine.
                                    —Unknown

20

There's a Song in the Air

*Suddenly a great company of the heavenly host
appeared with the angel, praising God. . . .*
—Luke 2:13

There's a Song in the Air

JOSIAH G. HOLLAND, 1819–1881   KARL P. HARRINGTON, 1861–1953

"Christmas Song"

1. There's a song in the air! There's a star in the sky! There's a moth-er's deep
2. There's a tu-mult of joy O'er the won-der-ful birth, For the Vir-gin's sweet
3. In the light of that star Lie the a-ges im-pearled; And that song from a-
4. We re-joice in the light, And we ech-o the song That comes down through the

prayer And a ba-by's low cry! And the star rains its fire while the
boy Is the Lord of the earth. Ay! the star rains its fire while the
far Has swept o-ver the world. Ev-ery hearth is a-flame, and the
night From the heav-en-ly throng. Ay! we shout to the love-ly e-

beau-ti-ful sing, For the man-ger of Beth-le-hem cra-dles a King!
beau-ti-ful sing, For the man-ger of Beth-le-hem cra-dles a King!
beau-ti-ful sing In the homes of the na-tions that Je-sus is King!
van-gel they bring, And we greet in His cra-dle our Sav-iour and King! A-MEN.

*W*hat a beautiful scene is drawn for us in this joyous Christmas hymn! As we visualize once more the glorious chorus of angels, the brilliant star, and Mary watching over her baby in the lowly manger, we feel like joining the "heavenly throng" in their "tumult of joy" in order to greet "our Savior and King!"

Josiah G. Holland created one of the most thoughtful and thrilling of all the carols of this season. It is no wonder that the angels' song rang out so jubilantly. They knew it was the King of heaven they were serenading. Did those who followed the brilliant light of the star realize, however, that through the ages the whole earth would be illuminated by Christ the Lord—"the bright Morning Star" (Rev. 22:16)? Like those who saw the guiding star, we too "rejoice in the light, and we echo the song. . . ."

> Glory to our God, we sing, Glory to our Lord and King;
> Peace, goodwill with all abide this holy Christmas tide.
> —A. L. Skoog

Josiah Holland began his professional career as a medical doctor and practiced for a short time in Springfield, Massachusetts. But soon he abandoned his medical practice and joined the editorial staff of the Springfield *Republican,* where be became well known as the writer of the "Timothy Titcomb Letters." Later he helped establish *Scribner's Magazine* and served as its editor until his death in 1881.

The present tune, "Christmas Song," was composed for these words by Karl P. Harrington approximately twenty-five years after the writing of the text. Harrington was a respected teacher of Latin in various leading universities. He was a member of several literary societies and was the author of a number of scholarly works. He was also a recognized musician, having served in various Methodist churches as organist and choir director. Harrington was one of the musical editors for the *Methodist Hymnal* of 1905.

"There's a Song in the Air" first appeared in a Sunday school collection in 1874 and five years later in Holland's *Complete Poetical Writings*. Its first inclusion in a church hymnal was in the *Methodist Hymnal* of 1905. It is still one of our choice Christmas songs and is worthy of much more notice than it normally receives.

———————————

Our day of joy is here again,
with love and peace and song;
Come, let us join th'angelic strain
with voices clear and strong.

Now to the manger let us go
to worship and adore
The tender Babe upon the straw,
our Savior evermore.

—*A. L. Skoog*

21

Thou Didst Leave Thy Throne

I have come that they may have life,
and have it to the full.

—John 10:10

Thou Didst Leave Thy Throne

EMILY E. S. ELLIOTT, 1836–1897   TIMOTHY R. MATTHEWS, 1826–1910

"Margaret"

1. Thou didst leave Thy throne and Thy king - ly crown When Thou
2. Heav - en's arch - es rang when the an - gels sang, Pro -
3. The fox - es found rest, and the birds their nest In the
4. Thou cam - est, O Lord, with the liv - ing word That should
5. When the heav'ns shall ring and the an - gels sing At Thy

cam - est to earth for me; But in Beth - le - hem's home was there
claim - ing Thy roy - al de - gree; But of low - ly birth didst Thou
shade of the for - est tree; But Thy couch was the sod, O Thou
set Thy peo - ple free; But with mock - ing scorn and with
com - ing to vic - to - ry, Let Thy voice call me home, say - ing,

found no room For Thy ho - ly na - tiv - i - ty. O
come to earth, And in great hu - mil - i - ty. O
Son of God, In the des - erts of Gal - i - lee. O
crown of thorn They bore Thee to Cal - va - ry. O
"Yet there is room—There is room at My side for thee." My

come to my heart, Lord Je - sus—There is room in my heart for Thee!
come to my heart, Lord Je - sus—There is room in my heart for Thee!
come to my heart, Lord Je - sus—There is room in my heart for Thee!
come to my heart, Lord Je - sus—There is room in my heart for Thee!
heart shall re - joice, Lord Je - sus, When Thou com - est and call - est for me!

*T*his spiritually enriching text differs from most Christmas songs in that it focuses not only on Jesus' birth but also on His life on earth, His suffering and death, and the ultimate triumph of His second coming.

This hymn by Emily Elliott was written to teach children the truths of the Advent and nativity seasons, especially the phrase from Luke 2:7, "because there was no room for them in the inn." The easily understood wording, the poetic imagery, and the spiritual truths found in these five stanzas soon made the text a widespread favorite of both young and old alike.

It is interesting to note in the first four stanzas the vivid contrasts emphasized by Miss Elliott between the exultation of Christ as the eternal God and His earthly humiliation as the Son of Man. Each contrasting statement within these verses begins with the word "but." Verse one compares the glories of Christ's pre-existence in heaven with His lowly entry into this world. The second stanza continues this contrast between our Savior's heavenly acclaim and His earthly rejection. The third stanza provides a descriptive difference between the provisions of shelter afforded even the lowly animals of the field with that which the Creator of the universe experienced throughout His earthly pilgrimage. The fourth stanza contains a most haunting truth: The One who left the glories of heaven to offer mankind eternal life received from man the shameful death on Calvary's cross.

As we contemplate the sobering truths of these four stanzas, we are moved to exclaim, "O come to my heart, Lord Jesus—there is room in my heart for Thee!" In the fifth stanza, however, the situation is reversed with the rejoicing at Christ's triumphant return and the prospect of being at His side throughout eternity.

Emily Elliott never married, but her life was filled with involvement in numerous religious causes and social concerns. She was known for her tireless efforts with rescue missions and in the Sunday school movement of that time. She also edited a children's magazine called the *Church Missionary Juvenile Instructor,* in which "Thou Didst Leave Thy Throne" was first published in 1864.

The tune, "Margaret" (taken from the Greek word meaning "pearl"), was composed especially for this text by an Anglican minister and musician, Timothy R. Matthews, twelve years after the words were written by Miss Elliott. The text and tune soon appeared together in a children's hymnal, *Children's Hymns and Tunes.*

This fine hymn has proved to be an inspiration for all ages, not only during the Christmas season, but also throughout the entire year.

---

*The coming of Christ at Christmas is in vain unless
we personally invite Him to dwell in our hearts
and to control our lives.*

*Order my footsteps by Thy Word,
And make my heart sincere;
Let sin have no dominion, Lord,
But keep my conscience clear.*
                    —*Unknown*

22

We Three Kings of Orient Are

After Jesus was born in Bethlehem in Judea,
during the time of King Herod, Magi from the east
came to Jerusalem and asked, "Where is the one
who has been born king of the Jews? We saw his
star in the east and have come to worship him."
Then they opened their treasures and presented him
with gifts of gold and of incense and of myrrh.
—Matthew 2:1–2; 2:11

We Three Kings of Orient Are

J. H. HOPKINS, 1820–1891   J. H. HOPKINS, 1820–1891

1. We three kings of O - ri - ent are; Bear - ing gifts we tra - verse a - far—
2. Born a King on Beth - le - hem's plain, Gold I bring to crown Him a - gain—
3. Frank - in - cense to of - fer have I; In - cense owns a De - i - ty nigh.
4. Myrrh is mine; its bit - ter per - fume Breathes a life of gath - 'ring gloom—
5. Glo - rious now be - hold Him a - rise— King and God and Sac - ri - fice.

Field and foun - tain, moor and moun - tain— Fol - low - ing yon - der star.
King for - ev - er, ceas - ing nev - er, O - ver us all to reign.
Prayer and prais - ing, all men rais - ing, Wor - ship Him, God on high.
Sor - r'wing, sigh - ing, bleed - ing, dy - ing, Sealed in the stone - cold tomb.
Al - le - lu - ia, al - le - lu - ia! Earth to heav'n re - plies.

Refrain

O star of won - der, star of night, Star with roy - al beau - ty bright,

West - ward lead - ing, still pro - ceed - ing, Guide us to thy per - fect light.

*A*ll of those involved in Christ's birth—Mary and Joseph, the innkeeper, the angels, the shepherds, and the wise men—have much to teach us. Although there is no scriptural basis for stating dogmatically that there were three wise men, the fact that three distinct gifts are mentioned has given rise to this ancient idea. Master artists throughout the centuries have depicted three wise men on camels as one of their favorite nativity themes. Tradition has also suggested that these three Magi were actually kings from the Orient with the names of Melchior, Caspar, and Balthazar.

The number of wise men is not important; all that really matters is that they persisted in following the light that was given them until they found the object of their search, that they responded in worship, and that they returned home to share their experience with others. Also, the gifts presented to the Christ child were both significant and appropriate: gold, symbolic of His kingly reign; frankincense, symbolic of His priestly ministry and oneness with the Father; and myrrh, symbolic of our redemption through His death. How important it is that our gifts of love, devotion, and service be offered to Christ after we have first found Him and then have bowed in true adoration before Him.

John Hopkins, the author and composer of this popular Christmas hymn, was an Episcopal minister who was also a seminary music teacher. He produced this dramatic carol in 1863 and has been credited with contributing much to the development of music in his denomination during the nineteenth century. One of his publications, *Carols, Hymns and Songs,* had four editions.

May we too follow the light of God's Word and the leading of His Holy Spirit as we bow in worship before Christ and give our lives to His service.

The star that rose at Bethlehem has never set.
It glows for those who seek its light. 'Tis leading yet.
They saw the star—and they alone—who longed for it.
For men like them the star that shone
        on Bethlehem will never set;
For those who come to Jesus' cross—'tis shining yet.

                                    —*Author unknown*

23

What Child Is This?

When they had seen him, they spread
the word concerning what had been told them
about this child.

—Luke 2:17

What Child Is This?

WILLIAM C. DIX, 1837–1898

Old English air

"Greensleeves"

Moderato *mf*

1. What Child is this, Who, laid to rest— On Ma-ry's lap— is sleep-ing? Whom
2. Why lies He in— such mean es-tate,— Where ox and ass— are feed-ing? Good
3. So bring Him in-cense, gold, and myrrh, Come peas-ant, king to own Him, The

an-gels greet with an-thems sweet, While shep-herds watch— are keep-ing?
Chris-tian, fear: for sin-ners here— The si-lent Word— is plead-ing:
King of kings sal-va-tion brings; Let lov-ing hearts en-throne Him.

REFRAIN *ff*

This, this— is Christ the King; Whom shep-herds guard— and an-gels sing:

Haste, haste to bring Him laud,—The Babe, the Son— of Ma-ry!

The question posed in this well-loved carol must have been upper-most in the minds of those present at Jesus' birth. We can almost hear the question being asked from one to another as they gazed into the humble manger. How difficult it must have been for them to understand that the Babe who lay in "such mean estate" was truly the long-awaited Messiah. And through the centuries men have continued to ponder who Christ really is—how can He be fully God and still fully man? Only through divine faith comes the revealed answer.

> He who is the Bread of Life began His ministry hungering.
> He who is the Water of Life ended His ministry thirsty.
> Christ hungered as man, yet fed the multitudes as God.
> He was weary, yet He is our rest.
> He prayed, yet He hears our prayers.
> He was sold for thirty pieces of silver, yet He redeems sinners.
> He was led as a lamb to the slaughter, yet He is the Good Shepherd.
> He died, and by dying destroyed death.
>
> —Author unknown

How forcefully the triumphant answer to this imposing question bursts forth in the refrain—"This, this is Christ the King."

This thoughtful text was written by William C. Dix, who was one of our finest lay hymn writers. As a successful insurance administrator in Glasgow, Scotland, he was stricken with a sudden serious illness at the age of twenty-nine. Dix was confined to bed for an extended period and suffered deep depression until he called out to God and "met Him in a new and real way." Out of this spiritual experience came more than forty artistic and distinctive hymns, including this delightful carol. It was taken from a longer Christmas poem, "The Manger Throne," written by Dix in 1865. He based this poem on the nativity account recorded in Matthew 2:1–12. Another well-known text by William Dix is the hymn "As with Gladness Men of Old." It is used especially during the Epiphany season, which begins January 6.

The melody "Greensleeves" is a traditional English folk tune of unknown origin. Through the years it has been associated with a great variety of texts. William Shakespeare noted in some of his plays that "Greensleeves" was a favorite tune of his day.

Who is He in yonder stall,
At whose feet the shepherds fall?
'Tis the Lord! O wondrous story!
'Tis the Lord! The King of Glory!
At His feet we humbly fall;
Crown Him! Crown Him! Lord of All!
            —Benjamin R. Hanby

24

While by Our Sheep

The shepherds returned, glorifying and praising God
for all the things they had heard and seen,
which were just as they had been told.

—Luke 2:20

While by Our Sheep

German carol

17th century carol

Trans. THEODORE BAKER–alt, 1851–1934

1. While by our sheep we watched at night, Glad tid-ings bro't an an - gel
2. There shall be born, so he did say, In Beth - le - hem a Child to -
3. There shall the Child lie in a stall, This Child who shall re - deem us
4. This gift of God we'll cher - ish well— Je - sus, our Lord Em - man - u -

bright:
day: How great our joy! (Great our joy!) Joy, joy, joy! (Joy, joy, joy!)
all:
el:

Praise we the Lord in heav'n on high! (Praise we the Lord in heav'n on high!)

*I*t was a cold, clear night. The stars twinkled above and an air of peaceful serenity settled calmly over the field outside of Bethlehem. The fire was burning low as the shepherds sprawled out to rest among their sheep. "What is the meaning of that star?" asked one of the younger boys. As some turned to look, the star seemed to sparkle with a glorious glow, almost hanging over Bethlehem. Then suddenly they were blinded by a brilliant light! They cried out in fright and hid their faces on the ground. The consoling voice of an angel calmed their spirits as they listened in rapture to the blessed announcement of the long-awaited Messiah. How great was their joy!

> Let us, like these good shepherds, then employ
> Our grateful voices to proclaim the joy;
> Trace we the Babe, who hath retrieved our loss,
> From His poor manger to the bitter Cross,
> Treading His steps, assisted by His grace,
> Till man's first heavenly state again takes place.
> —John Byrom

Have you ever wondered why these simple, uncouth shepherds without wealth, power, or social position were the first to receive heaven's glorious message? Prophecy foretold that salvation would be offered first to Israel. Thus the Jewish shepherds were allowed to adore the Savior before the arrival of the Gentile wise men. Perhaps the humble shepherds were also chosen to receive the angels' message because God wanted to send His only Son to be associated with the seemingly unimportant of this world rather than with the proud and wealthy. Also God knew that these lowly shepherds would receive His news of salvation with open hearts and would return with great joy to share what they had heard and seen.

This traditional German carol is thought to have originated in the seventeenth century. It was possibly used as part of a church drama with its offstage echo. The translator, Theodore Baker, was a German-born scholar who later became the literary editor for the G. Schirmer Company in New York from 1892–1926.

There is always joy when Jesus reigns, whether in earth or heaven, and the more complete His supremacy the deeper the joy.

---

*Take your place with the shepherds as the heavenly
announcement is given. Move with them to the manger
and worship in awe. Return with the song of praise
upon your lips. Hear the gentle echo in the night's stillness.
Share your joy with others.*

25

While Shepherds Watched Their Flocks

But the angel said to them, "Do not be afraid.
I bring you good news of great joy that will be
for all the people."

—Luke 2:10

While Shepherds Watched Their Flocks

NAHUM TATE, 1652–1715   GEORGE F. HANDEL, 1685–1759

*T*he singing of hymns such as we know today was practically non-existent in England and the United States, from the beginning of the sixteenth century Protestant Reformation until the dawn of the eighteenth century. During this time congregational singing consisted almost entirely of versified settings of the Psalms. The Psalter used exclusively during this period was the *Sternhold-Hopkins Psalter,* published in 1562. Though this Psalter was known for its faithfulness to the original Hebrew, the crude, unpoetic character of its texts became increasingly offensive to many congregations.

Finally, in 1696, during the reign of William and Mary, two Irishmen, Nahum Tate and Nicholas Brady, collaborated in undertaking a new metrical version of the Psalms to make them more in keeping with the literary tastes of the day. This new Psalter, known as the *New Version,* was met with widespread resistance at first. With the official endorsement by King William III, the *New Version* eventually replaced the old *Sternhold-Hopkins* throughout the Church of England. From England it came to America, where it was adopted by the American Episcopal Church in 1789. In 1700, Tate and Brady had already published a supplement to their *New Version.* The supplement contained sixteen hymns in addition to the metrical Psalms. One of these original hymns was Tate's Christmas carol description of the angels' appearance to the shepherds as described in Luke 2:8–14. It was titled "While Shepherds Watched Their Flocks." All of Tate's other hymns from this collection have since been forgotten.

Nahum Tate was born in Dublin in 1652, the son of an Irish clergyman. He was educated at Trinity College and in 1690 was proclaimed the

Poet Laureate of England for the court of William and Mary during their reign from 1689–1702. Unfortunately, Tate's professional achievements sharply contrasted with his private life. A fondness for drink coupled with unwise spending habits eventually led to his downfall, and he died at the age of sixty-three in a debtors' refuge in London, England.

"While Shepherds Watched Their Flocks" ranks as one of our most popular Christmas carols and is found in nearly every church hymnal. Its purely narrative account about the shepherds is on a level that even small children can visualize and understand easily. The music for this carol has been adapted from a work by master musician George Frederick Handel, best known for his oratorio, the *Messiah,* composed in 1741 and completed in just twenty-four days.

Break forth, O beauteous heav'nly light,
and usher in the morning;
You shepherds, shrink not with affright,
but hear the angel's warning.
This Child, now weak in infancy,
our confidence and joy shall be,
The pow'r of Satan breaking,
our peace eternal making.

—Johann Rist

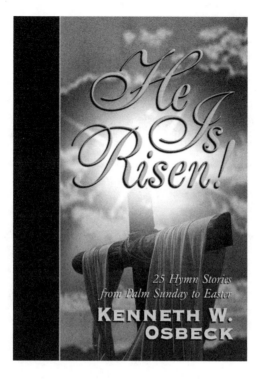

He Is Risen!
(Available spring '99)

This collection of hymn stories adds depth to the Easter season and throughout the year by following Jesus' journey from His triumphal entry into Jerusalem to His death on the cross and His victory over the grave.

Each story includes the inspiration behind the writing of a hymn, devotional thoughts for meditation, Scripture verses appropriate to the season, and the complete musical score. Some of the hymns included are

- "Christ the Lord Is Risen Today"
- "Jesus Paid It All"
- "My Jesus, I Love Thee"
- "O Sacred Head, Now Wounded"
- "The Old Rugged Cross"

0-8254-3432-7   112 pages

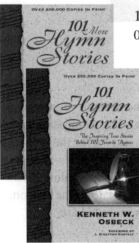